A Dollhouse Built on Brimstone

A Dollhouse Built on Brimstone

Lucas Daliah Galvin

Black Napkin Press
2017

A Dollhouse Built on Brimstone
Copyright © 2017 by Lucas Daliah Galvin

Published by Black Napkin Press
Huntington Beach, CA
http://www.black-napkin-press.com

Cover Art: Carley Smith

All rights reserved. No part of this book may be reproduced or transmitted in any form or by any means without written permission from the author or publisher.

ISBN-13: 978-0-9974465-1-7
ISBN-10: 0-9974465-1-X

"In a dream you saw a way to survive and you were full of joy."
—Jenny Holzer

"It is myself I have never met whose face is pasted on the underside of my mind please open the curtains."
—Sarah Kane

TABLE OF CONTENTS

I AM A HIGH SCHOOL NEED FOR VALIDATION	1
AS THOUGH A BREATHING EXERCISE COULD CURE ME OF MY CHILDHOOD	4
GENESIS	6
SAGITTARIUS RISING	8
MANIC PIXIE NIGHTMARE QUEER	11
THERAPY BURNOUT	13
A BOUQUET OF OLEANDER	15
CATHOLIC GUILT, MY FAIRWEATHER FRIEND	19
OUR BONES ARE STREAKED WITH THE WORST OF IT	21
I USED TO MAKE YOU LAUGH…	25
LOST BOY / GOOD GIRL	26
AN ENTIRE CHAPBOOK ABOUT US WILTING	28
POST BREAK UP SEX	32
VACANT AND CONDEMNED	34
HELLFIRE	38
EAST COUNTY	40
STILL THAWING, FOREVER FRIGID	44
CAN YOU BE BOTH THE EXHIBITIONIST AND THE VOYEUR	46
ANOTHER FALSE DICHOTOMY	47
TO THE HIDDEN SMOKE SPOTS OF UCSD	49
SIX BEERS DEEP	50
DYSPHORIA! AT THE PARTY	53
HEAVY SLEEPER	55
REPENTANCE IN THE DIRT	57
IN ANY TIMELINE, I DESERVED BETTER	60
I AM HELLFIRE	61
NOTHING GOOD COMES FROM BEING GONE	62
CAFFIENE FUELED RECOVERY	65

I AM A HIGH SCHOOL NEED FOR VALIDATION

they ask,
when did i
become
so grown up?

i swallow back
laughter like
shards of glass

this did not happen
with my permission

i am no longer
skinned knees
and loose teeth

i shuffle through
past versions of myself
like a deck of tarot cards
bent at the edges
still trying to glean
meaning from the
faded images,
deciphering the
past through
other people's
interpretations
of my present:

the psychologist
and her fancy
words for
"starved for love" and
"middle child syndrome"

my past lovers
and their
misguided attempts
in believing i was
a thing needing rescuing

you
and your
fucking terrifying
belief
that there is
more to me
than my fractured
schemas

my brother once
asked what
could i possibly know
about myself if
i've never been in a fight?

the bruises on his knuckles
promise he is very self-assured
i do not know how
to analyze the
violet blossoms in my chest

i have been wed to
the tragedy flowing
through my veins,
my trauma
has become
my biology
i am fighting
to divorce myself
from the home
i built in my mourning
to salvage
some semblance
of identity

in the wreckage
they made of me
maybe once i was
a victim
but now
oh my God
i don't know
who i am

AS THOUGH A BREATHING EXERCISE COULD CURE ME OF MY CHILDHOOD

my feet are bare
as i draw my bruised
knees to my chest
on the bathroom counter
interrogating my reflection
waiting for a flicker of recognition
i am an excess of scar tissue
scabs on my knuckles
hysterical mascara tears
and gourmet vomit
all angles and skipped meals
playing the role of someone else
in a hand-me-down leather jacket
hollow eyes reflect my own
my body is foreign territory to me
i could not pick myself out of a crowd
men have always been drawn to me
how sugar brings bugs crawling
the way that beasts
smell fear
my mother blames the
fluttering of my eyelashes
as though she is not the one
who taught me to wield
my beauty like a weapon
taught me to lie down for
the Father
offering my petals like communion
wafers on sinners' tongues
i resent my own softness

how *no* never found its
way into my vocabulary
it is my own repulsion
that curdles in my stomach
my family is full of

karma Houdinis
that slip from jail
cells
wriggling out of
charges and sentences
their shame is my own
carried in my lungs
like pond water
i drown in my sleep
in my dreams of
teeth and bones
my forehead leans
against the cool glass
of the mirror
streaked with
toothpaste spit
i wonder how
the shards of glass
would feel in my
palms
if the sting would
bring me out of this
trance
i still catch
traces of her
in my features
and i wonder
if her ghost
still lingers
and if she
knows
that i do not blame her

GENESIS

there are conflicting
accounts of your
birth

you were spat out by
a glistening cloud
of gnats

you tumbled out of
a pumpkin patch

you were left for dead
in aisle ten

you were not ejected
from the hexed womb
of a bruised woman

she devoured the love
you offered her
on a suburban altar
to heal those wounds
she had inflicted on
the both of you

you rewrite your
backstory
every night behind
closed eyes

your home is
nowhere
your family is
no one

you are a wisp of smoke
a wraith
a pile of cherry pits

there is a scrapbook
she kept with pictures
of your true origins
and you wonder if
she traces the edges
and wonders

where
are
you
now?

SAGITTARIUS RISING

summer holds a
stagnant sadness
that would taste almost sweet
were it not so heavy

trickles down my throat
to settle in my stomach
like syrup
as warm as cough medicine
i no longer fight it

draw the curtains
shut
knees to my chest
ignore both the
sunlight fighting
to filter in through
the flimsy blinds
and the memories
woven in each passing
hour

i paint my walls in kerosene
and invite Despair and all her
lit matches in

"there are worse
things than someone loving you,
you know"
she had warned me
between drags on her cigarettes

well, Mother,
there is love
and there is
consumption
bared teeth

devouring
young flesh
wide-eyed
held breaths

where were you to
tell me the difference?

Mother,
there is maternity
and there is
gaslighting
coaxing them
into
your reality

liar—put on your strappy shoes
liar—where did you get that bruise
liar—that never happened

and there you were
hurting me for my
own good

holding my head
beneath the water
naïve lungs
punished
for the crime
of growing in the
wrong womb

i sleep away the
months rife
with daylight hoping to forget

Mother there
are worse things than remembering
nostalgia is heavy
nostalgia is sweet

i still see you smoking
your cigarettes on the
sunken porch
your unkempt patch of
wild dahlias

there are
worse things than
being loved

MANIC PIXIE NIGHTMARE QUEER

to every boy
that has fallen for
all the empty words
i've spun from thin air
like candy floss

the boys
who became infatuated
with a ghost of a person
that never quite existed

sad boys
who decided
i was nothing more than
a plot device
in their respective indie drama

to the boys
that have made
me feel more like
a supporting role,
a manic pixie wet dream
than an actual person:

you have exploited me
for the sake of your own
tragedy porn

you cannot pretend i'm delicate
and expect me to rescue you
from your troubled art school ennui

you found a home in
my sickness
like a stranger peering out
at a car wreck
invading someone else's

moment of catastrophe
hijacking pain that is not yours
yet walked away when you
realized my disorder was
chronic and more than
an aesthetic

i refuse to soothe your wounds
i will be the salt
the next time you choose to use me

i am not your cure

THERAPY BURNOUT

my nightmares are for me to decipher
no one else has any business
sifting through those ashes

my therapist says, fat is not an emotion
what am i really feeling?

the cognitive model argues that
our thoughts fuel our emotions
which in turn control our behavior

this is not how i am supposed to be
but devastation pumps through my veins,
with this curse i have inherited
how was i supposed to turn out any different?

i want to tell her, my feelings
are nightshade, bitter on my tongue
my thoughts
a churning sea that
i have grown tired of treading

my behaviors
are my bad habits
i hold in my throat,
carry in my pocket
the only lens through
which i can catch a
glimpse of myself

fat is not an emotion
but how do i explain
to this not yet jaded woman
that this fear is my constant,
that threat of excess flesh
an enmeshed part of my identity

who would i be without
praying to my caloric deficit?

leave me to sputter on those ashes
these nightmares are the sickness
i reside in
without them i would be transient

A BOUQUET OF OLEANDER

I.
turning over stones to
expose the creatures
lurking underneath
trying to find out
who are you, really?

divorcing yourself from the half truths
your mother crafted to supplement
her own propaganda
proving herself
ironclad and impervious

the fantasies she spun
unravel in your hands
stories woven
to paint herself as the
selfless feminine,
the merciful blood Mother
not the martyr, the victim,
the sadist, the monster
who taught you that
fear and love leave
the same metallic
aftertaste in your mouth

fractured memories
and forbidden histories
float downstream
growing murky
with the algae bloom
pooling around your ankles

where does she end
and where do you begin?

II.
the past is over
but you still
feel it living
in the remnants
left behind
staining the whorls
of your fingertips

she still visits you
in waves of tears
on public transit
and glimpses in
stained mirrors
her eyes staring
back at you

even now she claims
ownership of you
your reflection is only
an extension of her

in photographs
you are her
thinner alter ego
painted lips
and scars
on your
pale thighs like
chips in fine china

though you are the fruit
that fell from her
unforgiving branches
you hope that she would
no longer recognize you
you have become
more sharp edges
than wilted petals
you are a minefield,

no longer that tender thing
she had mangled
because she could
and this frightens her

it never occurred to her
that it scares you too

you are no longer small enough
to fit the coffin she had built
she did not know how to love
something she could not control

you are both
the color blue
unfathomable and vast

she is
hypothermia,
frozen Atlantic
ocean death

you are warm and pure
as a southern sky
in spring time
untouched by
her biting chill

one day, i promise you
that you will look in the mirror
and see only yourself

CATHOLIC GUILT, MY FAIRWEATHER FRIEND

Catholic guilt has a funny way
of rearing it's ugly head
whenever i start to feel safe
yet is nowhere to be found
when i swallow my Abilify
by the handful like this
loathing is a contest

i can sum up the
perpetual bruising of my knees
in a single religious motif
with clasped hands
squeezing my eyes shut
whispering
please don't tell, please don't tell

all my mothers have been martyrs
in one way or another
and their tears scald my flesh
a hot angry scarlet

the bright-eyed counseling intern
at the hospital asks me to imagine
my illness as a third-party entity
and not a Hell i carry in the space
behind my ribs

and i see my Despair personified
as some scrawny kid with golden hair
and tired eyes, snot crusted over
their sleeves

the monsters i have been warned of
look too much like me

OUR BONES ARE STAINED WITH THE WORST OF IT

fucked up kids
have a way of finding each other
we wear our mothers' shame like strands
of inherited pearls around our necks,
our fathers' temper trembling in our hands.
the sky is a raw bruise
tinged with light pollution
from too many strip malls
and sprawled out in her
back seat i cannot see a single
star
no one has touched me
without adding lye to
my shallow creeks
and i cannot help
but wonder if the
writhing turns her on
the thrill has long since
faded from knowing
when someone wants
to fuck me
it is the same look
of longing
that reminds me
exactly where i come from

her hand is traveling up my
skirt and i know
she thinks she can
silence the tragedies that
sing in our veins
replenish what was stolen
when our mothers'
backs were turned
but between her thighs
i am forgiven
my throat is a shallow grave

of *no* and *stop*
whenever i try to spit it out
it lodges itself
there like a threat
to myself
anytime someone
tries to show me
i deserve to feel good
the best moments in my life
are the worst
both lust and regret
leave my tongue
slick with the same
taste

I USED TO MAKE YOU LAUGH BUT NOW
I JUST DEPRESS THE FUCK OUT OF YOU
(YOU CAUGHT ONE GLIMPSE OF MY HELL
AND DECIDED TO GO HOME)

here is a wound
that i am still
bleeding from
that may have
healed already
had i left the
scab alone
but i am all
nervous habits
and restless energy
so i pick
and pick
and pick
until the better parts of me
unravel and give way
to familial mythos
my Mother had warned
me not to air my dirty
laundry out in public
hold my history a secret
lodged in my throat
keep them all guessing
at arm's length
you don't say it
but i know that you
find me at my most beautiful
when i am
draped in layers of denial
when my edges are softened,
empty half-truths down
your throat like codeine
warming you from the inside
but i wanted to toss my booze back

like a champion drinker
surrender to the concept
that i am past saving
my mother had ditched this
abysmal state altogether,
left no forwarding address
where was she
to warn me of the
hungry purveyors
of tragedy porn, the
bridges the truth would burn?
here is a wound grown infected
that i refuse to dress
and i do nothing
of my serrated edges
i was born beneath a bad sign
into a family that was never mine
that house was built on brimstone
and truth was the match threatening
to swallow us in flames
the doctor just wants to do his job
and i am making it difficult
i could tell him, i was just a kid
i could tell him, it wasn't once or twice
i could tell him, it was every day
but what dosage of any chemical
could rewrite history
the fact is, it was at least fifty times
the fact is, i remember the taste
the fact is, no one wants to hear about it
you are keeping me anchored here
with your worried glances
the "i'm just trying to help you" routine
you look so damn desperate when you ask
if i am trying to die
but know the answer already
my brain distorts everything around me
i cannot fathom the fact that i am
not as disgusting as i was taught
your love is hard to comprehend

i am starved for it yet
drowning in it would never be enough
it slips through my fingers
before i can grasp it
the doctor is looking at me funny
the way they always do
"well, did you tell anyone?"
i was only a child
i was never a child
i tried
what else is there to say
fragile is not the same as innocent
this shame is as much mine as it is his
i am complicit, what don't you fucking get?
guilty, no trial, life sentence
he rips off a sheet from his pad
a new running gag between us
i will make a mess of things
and they will prescribe a cure
so no one will have to hear me
confess that
he stole from me
every day
next to the kitchen table
and my knees were always raw from the friction
and then i would have to eat there every night
and maybe that's where i lost my appetite
the first and last time
i have had enough misguided pity
to last me a goddamn lifetime
and i never want to make eye contact
with someone with good intentions again
i'll take your repulsion a thousand times over
before i let you apologize for my pathetic past
i want to unravel,
a slurring mess in your lap,
wide-eyed and wanting
use me use me
forget i ever told you anything
fucking destroy me

my body can be yours too
but you're giving me that look again
you're picturing me in the assessment room
again with my flesh gaping beneath my sleeves
your hands beneath my shirt
counting my ribs in your head again
i am killing both of us again
i don't get what *help* means
my mother told me to shut my fucking mouth
and i never listened
remember when i used to make you laugh?
it's different now, i'm sorry

LOST BOY / GOOD GIRL

i am both the doctor and the patient
breaking confidentiality
coaxing my head into
something close enough
to better off than dead
flushing the acrid taste of
my own fucked schemas
from my mouth with
booze i parted
my thighs for like
a lukewarm invitation
to stir me from my sleep

i could fall in love with a boy with hands like that
this is not the first time
someone has wrapped them around my throat
asked if i liked being choked
scar tissue spelling out
victim

i could fall in love with a girl with a name like that
she burns bridges
to keep only herself warm
she does not belong to anyone
but something inside me is stirring
at the sight of her in my leather jacket

i wish it was wired in me
to be delicate

take me cream and two sugars
and i will still burn going down

i depend on women to soothe my wounds
and men to split them back open again
let your body be my coffin
i don't mind feeling spent

AN ENTIRE CHAPBOOK ABOUT US WILTING

a vain attempt to coax your
stubborn stomach into
holding more than a mug
or three of too strong coffee
ends up swirling down the
drain in acidic chunks
with no one to tell you
to clear your plate
you do not bother
here are forty ounces
warm as tears
streaming smooth and salty
down your pallid cheeks
we swap the bottle back
and forth and i do not
comment on your
translucence
though i feel if
you were to let me
touch you
my fingers would
go through

your body is a
vacant lot
and neither of us
know how to keep
the other warm
i would let you crawl
inside me
if i wasn't so damn cold
i would cover the tab for
our joint funeral
you tell me that
i ought to get some sleep
but i never surrender
to my melatonin

in fear that you might
leave before the moonlight
gives way to the unforgiving sun
and when we both roll
out of bed for a class
we might as well just skip
our untouched breakfast gets
scraped into the trash

POST BREAK UP SEX

i was wearing my
favorite worn, soft flannel
more goldenrod than yellow
the color of the mustard
they use at good restaurants

your room was just as you
had left it the last time
you said *i love you*
and meant it

you were too beautiful
for me to believe
anything you said
i don't know what you saw in me
other than the fact that
i could make you laugh
and that i knew how to shuffle words around
elegantly enough for you to feel safe
for a moment at least

i do not know what you saw
in me now
only that you should not be looking
and i should not be in here
but i am
and it makes me nervous
how easily i feel comfortable
on your bed again
head resting on your floral pillowcase
smudged with eyeliner

your hot pink
hello kitty stereo
playing the CD i had
mixed for you months ago
covered in Lisa Frank

unicorn stickers
Ben Gibbard's voice
taunting me from
across the room
and i wondered if our
freckles would still
be perfectly aligned

the words trailed out
your mouth slow
and sweet
as your cat curled up
on my bare chest

last saturday
i had been with someone
not you
it was rough but it was honest
and it made me feel empty
and it made me feel cheap
i got to the concert
twenty minutes late
with swollen lips sticky
with blood
and dark hickies on my
ashen flesh
when i wandered in to the
bathroom my
whirlpool eyes were sunken and
too big
and instead of slamming my head
through the glass i just laughed
and went into the pit

your fingers graze the
bruises on my ribs
and you asked
"where does it hurt"

and i said
here
here
and here

and you kissed it all better
i fell for you again like
a kid knees first
skidding on gravel
off of the swings

it was a mess of
Nars lipstick
and stolen red wine
a lesson in being
tender
if not completely
reckless

but it is the
warm spring air
drifting in through the
screen,
it is the season
of eternal sunshine
making the same mistakes
over
and
over
and over

your fingers tangled in
my hair
i tell you what you want to hear
and when you fall asleep
i check your pulse and
the rise and fall of your chest
leave a glass of water

slightly buzzed
i hop back on my bicycle
and make my way back home
the bandage ripped from a wound
i am still bleeding from but
something in my chest
is still humming

VACANT AND CONDEMNED

my body is the house
i grew up in
and periodically
attempt to burn down
my wooden floors rotting
as the wallpaper peels
there are bugs in the sink
and more mildew than paint
on the ceiling
this is the house
with the sagging porch
where i gave myself away
the first, the second
the fiftieth time
knees scrubbed raw
with friction
feeling the absence of
something not yet defined
here are the rooms
in the summer where
you can hear the bees
humming outside
and feel the humid
upstate air wrap
around you like a blanket,
mouth sticky from more
blue raspberry Popsicles
then mom said you could have
here is the yard
the expanse of forest
and meadow
where you
stood too small, wondering
breathless and trembling
if the yawning earth could
swallow you whole
this is the house

haunted by everyone who
has come and gone
and come back again,
those that traipsed
through so suddenly
that without the
phantom echoing
down the hallway
you are not so sure
they were here at all
i throw rocks through
the already broken
windows
and scream,
demanding answers
cursing the very ground
this wretched cold
home was built on
i fall to my knees
in the front yard
overgrown with
dandelions and
clover
and whisper
thank you
thank you
thank you

HELLFIRE

tired of
fair bones
and lace
girls decaying
in the dark,
pretty words
for vomit

writing odes
to the ache
in my joints,
the scalding of
my throat

singing to
my ugly,
cradling it close

want to know what
light feels like
as it
splinters bones

i may be more
ash
than fire
but
i am ready to
devour
i will
force you
from your home

i am the
ugly sister
who can
deafen entire
rooms

without parting
my lips

i am the
heathen
corrupting your
daughters
with the
parting
of my thighs

i part entire seas
and swallow them
as easy as the
mint ice cream
i purge hunched
over the garbage
disposal,
those grinding
metal parts

i am a
wayward daughter,
a mouthful of
canker sores
flirting with salt
and Hellfire
i will
gouge myself
from the inside
before i become
your shrinking violet

my too broad shoulders
will split the seams
of the fragility you're
projecting on me,
this black-and-white
glamour-shot martyrdom—
you can see the light

shine through
their translucent
veils of flesh but
a photograph
can't betray
the stench of sickly
sweet ketosis piss

i am a book of matches,
taste
the gasoline
on my teeth
taste
the dying things
i bury behind my
angles and curves
taste
the
vehement
blood coursing
through my veins
the beating of my heart
that says
i am here
i am here

know that i am not
yet buried

remind me of this
with your fingertips
remind me of this
with your bones
against mine
remind me
that
i am a fire
that knows
more than
destruction

and
consumption
but how to carry warmth
and
feel
how it rages
how it sparks
for you
for you
for you

EAST COUNTY

we were all
motherless children

our only dream
throughout our
too loud childhoods
anywhere but here

we put
as many freeway
exits between us
and the past
as we could afford

a neon sprawl in the dust
a computer chip in some
abandoned machine

liquor store
7-Eleven
strip club
gas station

nestled in a
threadbare neighborhood
overlooking
the mouth of a canyon
where the kids
smoke their stale weed
and coyotes stalk unlucky cats

shining amber creatures
emerge from torn floral wallpaper
as the daylight fights to pour in through
heavy wooden blinds
but barely trickles in
the whole place smells

of damp clothes and bong water

it is still and it is quiet
we relish the silence
scarf it down with
hurried hands
the way i would
steal my sister's
Halloween candy when
she was in the shower
the subsequent sugar
comedown, the belly ache

sometimes i take home
samples of my
Mother's old perfume
just to feel that familiar
pang of panic

STILL THAWING, FOREVER FRIGID

carrying the weight of every
New England winter
the tangled bare
branches
upstate
this time of year
is frigid, formidable

a carousel
of chemical remedies
each with their own
side effects
nothing swelling the
emptiness shut
nothing smoothing
the serrated edges
of my thoughts

it is the very
core of my being
that needs to be
dismantled
it is the very fabric
of my being
that needs to be
untangled

therapists
bright-eyed interns
tattered converse
Neiman Marcus blouse
smart shoes
too bright teeth

lying by omission
they
offer the same

empty encouragement,
promising what
they would know is
false and frankly
unattainable
had they read my file

that same look of pity,
regarding me silently
as this mangled thing,
a thicket of scar tissue
layers of frost in a heated room

(every time i am called strong
i am really being told
i will fail
and it is only through
these subliminal meanings
that i can salvage something
close to truth
and this is not helpful
and this is not what i need
and this is not safe anymore
i will freeze to death and back
again)

frigid, formidable
branches intertwined
with my ribs
threatening to splinter
apart

inhale, exhale
choking back winter
my fingertips are numb
again
i'm kissing with my
eyes open
again

absence makes the heart grow
fonder
fondness made this heart grow
softer
overripe and tender
as love is an organic thing
that death can touch
as love is something that can and
will rot

i read your letters but your heart
is no longer in the ink
those words no longer writhe

and i think about
who was here
before you
and who will
be there
after me

the tenuous links
between
love and lover,
there you go
walking off with
my history
with someone
who will soon
walk off with
yours as well

i carry the cumulative
weight
of every Syracuse
snowfall

there are parts of me
that will not thaw
there is flawed chemistry

in my brain that will not
realign
there is distance i cannot
swell shut

i will freeze to death and
back again

CAN YOU BE BOTH THE EXHIBITIONIST AND THE VOYEUR? (MYFREECAMS VOTES YES)

made sixty-two dollars
sprawled across

my tangled Star Wars sheets

in the little blue light of my
laptop baring whatever self i
have left for strangers

who feel entitled to those scraps,
those starved dogs hounding the
dinner table

i strip myself for you down
to stained bone baring
fragile blood vessels that
exact kind of emotional

exhibitionism you have become
a purveyor of

as i place my fingers
between my legs

it feels awfully like
slamming car doors shut

on brittle bone
the chat room
is filled with
faster, baby
harder, baby

you're so hot, baby

and i know i shouldn't like
it, but it feels a lot like

losing my
virginity in a
parking lot on one
of those
summer nights

where i can almost confuse
the light pollution orange
glow of the sky for
something beautiful

ENMESHMENT

a long line of
amorphous performances
i myself am convoluted

who am i
who am i
who am i

a bruised apple that
never fell far
from the tree

a delayed
reaction to
abandonment
only now
five years later
do i dare act out

who am i rebelling against
by burning the home
that never
knew warmth?

painting my face
with the ashes,
i remain unrecognized
and this is relief
and this is uncertainty

once i was
a comma-shaped
egg alongside
your thigh
and we
were never
apart

ANOTHER FALSE DICHOTOMY

here is Girl as
failed attempts at
trophy daughter,
a blurred experience
that will forever be on my resumé
here are my bones stained
with Girl
her calcium deficiencies
her meals of ash and
coffee grounds
Girl disappearing into herself as
Girl has a tendency to do
here is Boy as scabbed knuckles
learning how to swing fists
instead of baring a
raw heart to salt
Boy demands to be heard
he has never owed an apology
for the space he takes up
Boy is not familiar
with the metallic taste
of biting your tongue to keep
quiet
i am not Boy
my voice is far too light
and dies in my throat,
a shallow graveyard of
yes
please
thank you
i am trying to translate
gray static into
something fathomable
using a language that
never considered the
possibility of Self
in the first place

Girl and Boy
like anything else
are only
coercion
and
performance

how much of myself
belongs to me
and no one else?

TO THE HIDDEN SMOKE SPOTS OF UCSD

she grows impatient,
readjusts my hands
around the sea glass
colored pipe

today is nearly yesterday
i'm putting tomorrow on hold
the smoke is a medicinal stench
sticking to my hair, my clothes
my lungs

the swings
at the park
too narrow for
my hips
and i get dizzier much
faster than before

weightlessness gives
way to headaches

i cough, indiscreet
the whole neighborhood
can smell what we are doing

there are things
i have
grown out of
in my sleep
yet
i have become
as stagnant
as the smoke
lazily dissipating
in the humid night

SIX BEERS DEEP

i used to dream of
drowning
and i still know
how to beg
but now
sleep is hunger
visiting
as a throbbing vein
in my neck
an unwelcome
gnawing in my stomach

we've got
bottles
and
we've got
cans
to blur the lines
where i end
and you begin
turning my
don't you dare
to
sure,
fine,
whatever

and i let you sink
your painted nails
in to my shoulders
hoping that the sight
of my own blood
will remind me
that i know better

i think of going under
just hold my head

beneath the water
and tell me like
you always do

you're hurting me for my own good
you're hurting me for my own good
you're hurting me for my own good

all 140 pounds of you
crushing me like
flower petals
beneath your heel
grind me into
the filthy pavement,
a used-up cigarette
you bummed from
someone else

would you still like me
if i didn't fall in to myself
to make room anymore?
would you still like me
if i didn't let you
consume me anymore?

there are shapes
my lips don't
want to make
places around
my teeth
my tongue won't go
sounds that
retreat down
my throat

would you still like me if
i stopped holding still?
would you still like me if
i said
no?

i think of going under
just hold my head
beneath the water
and tell me like
you always do

you're hurting me for my own good
you're hurting me for my own good
you're hurting me for my own good

you're hurting me

i used to think about dying
but now i just think about fucking
either way it's
your hands
around
my throat

DYSPHORIA! AT THE PARTY

i'm a drunk kid
reconciling Catholic
guilt in too many
bathroom breaks
picking at scabs
hoping to unravel
into a pile of
something that cannot
be salvaged

our lips sticky with
bad weekdays dissolving
into worse mistakes

i'm a fucking novelty
settling some bet
you have going with
drunken curiosity
i am playing along
my heart an ugly tangle
of desperation for
someone, anyone
aspartame on my tongue
empty but close enough

you ask
if i'm a real boy
your hands pressed
against my bound
chest
and i tell you
as the room tilts
slurring betraying my
bottled bravado
i can be whatever
you want me to be

you had called me
he and him
at the start of the evening
but now
tangled up in someone else's
bed sheets
you whisper a confession
that you have never been
with a girl before

nothing has been reconciled
no compromise settled
between the gnawing
in my gut
and the reeling in my head

i am your new
flavor for the week
trial-size sample
of something you will
never use again
but will recommend
to your friends

does this
turn you on?

HEAVY SLEEPER

i drifted through the
defining moments of my life
in unceremonious, dreamless sleep
like the first baby tooth that i ever lost
gulped down with warm milk
and graham cracker crumbs
there are no stamps in my passport
despite where i have been
no way to draw a coherent line
from point a or point b
or track how momentous
or stunted my growth has been
through the years

in fact, there is no evidence
to suggest that i have existed
anywhere at all
my heart is stagnant but you drag it
with you like gum on your shoe,
i am the ink stains on your fingers
the only proof that i am here
the traces of myself that you smear
across the page

alternatively, i could very well be
on my way to Hell
i say i'm already there
out of some
ironic sense of
self-preservation
but i am not sure that i truly
understand what eternal damnation
even means, if i could begin to grasp
how long an eternity lasts if i cannot
even comprehend the fact that two
decades have slipped through my fingers
would i even recognize my own immortal soul

if i can't even pick myself out of a crowd?

i am no one and i am nowhere
but one day i hope that you will
be the one to wake me up
and stamp my passport for me
to prove that we are capable
of inhabiting a corporeal plane
together, occupying space
within one another
that we are capable
of settling like water in
sorry lungs for more than
a fleeting moment that will
pass like medicated sleep

REPENTANCE IN DIRT

i am becoming repetitious
the crumpled paper littering
the floor as trite as my
shifts in mood
that no one else can notice
but my tired psychiatrist
warning me to slow down

it goes like this:
my nervous energy
shaking hands with
springtime's recklessness
binging on daylight
the rush of hypomania after
a two-month depressive spell

drinking a pot of coffee
on an empty stomach
wine out of paper cups
in the park with friends
every cell in my body
buzzing with life
after weeks of starving in
a coffin my own flawed
chemistry
had wrought

i fall in like-like with everybody
who bares an inch of
authenticity
my chest hums when i
catch glimpses of the
intricacies of someone else
the rush of recognizing parts
of yourself in others
reminding you that you are
not alone here

or the high of witnessing
something you had never
considered could exist
in another person

i fall in love with
this and that so
quickly that it
feels like a car crash
where everyone survives
but only by a breath
my heart swells with
the cacophony of it all
gnarled metal and melted plastic
it blurs my ability
to make normal decisions
i feel the need to consume
it all before the next
episode starts descending

i am a clueless kid
a fledgling adult
with a surplus of love
to give and far too
eager to get
punched in the face
in a parking lot

tell me what songs
make you feel alive
tell me about your childhood
i want to know about the words
that keep you going
i want to know what kind of kid
you were
i want to memorize your backstreets
so i can find you with my eyes closed

my palms sweat more these days
i want to fill my lungs with dirt

let flowers bloom from my chest
my feelings are the sea churning
with exposed nerves and too
much salt

no one taught me how to observe
quietly
instead i devour and demolish
what i long to be part of
maybe next month i will apologize
for not knowing when to slow down
and for tracking mud on your
mopped floors
but for now
there is dirt beneath my nails
and caked on my boots
my head is shaved
and i am just as i want to be

filthy and free and full of love
to give away

IN ANY TIMELINE, I DESERVED BETTER

consider the following:
some alternate timeline
alarming and absurd
in its implication that
i would ever call you again
or even more so
that you would pick up at all
in which we were both
more forgiving
and my legs spread
like an invitation
you feel the need to
remind me that my eyes
are amber
and you do not leave in the morning
in which my body is not a crime scene
it is something still alive
and capable of passion
i am no longer a grave
you hold your breath past
nothing is broken
there is no crunch of
tiny bones
between the jaws
of something darker
consider the following:
i know the bottles
are hiding in plain sight
in the dark on a shelf
behind a locked door
i can open with a swipe
of my expired library card
i do not need to
in any universe,
shattered parts
eventually
heal themselves

I AM HELLFIRE

i am tired of
fair bones
and lace
girls decaying
in the dark,
pretty words
for vomit

you may
think i am waning,
more
ash
than fire
but
i am ready to
devour,
to scorch the hills and
force you from your home

i am dangerous,
can't you taste
the gasoline
on my teeth?

NOTHING GOOD COMES FROM BEING GONE

spent the years
attempting to perfect
my disappearing act

punishing my body
for the crime of not
being
small
smaller
smallest

as though
shedding flesh
can reclaim
the purity
i had given away

as though i could
become intangible,
become light itself
and fade away

a prolonged
exit scene
dragged out
long enough
to rid itself
of theatrics

my cumulative
attempts
at becoming
a ghost
have been
a failure

the part of me
i have not buried
with what you have
touched
celebrates this
failure with
everything, everything

this is the
part of me
that still has
defiance
memorized
that knows how to
bite and kick
that walks
with heavy
steps
and pierces the
still air
with clouds
of breath
to prove that
i can occupy space

i am not
the perpetual
Listerine sweetness
of my mouth
nor the acrid
remnants of meals
i fought to skip

i refuse to be
a good victim
anymore
i will not be your martyr

i am here
i am here
i am here

learning to pray
to what has made me
stranger and harder to love
taking a moment to
respect the
holy
devastation site
i have become

CAFFEINE FUELED-RECOVERY

your haircut
your bad grades
your messy room
your skinned knees
your sloppy handwriting
you are a gross kid,
a messy kid,
a three-months-of-
unfinished-homework-
hidden-in-your-closet kid
even today you eat fruit
after noticing the wispy
dandelion fuzz of mold,
you wipe your nose
on your sleeve
you wear the same binder
weeks on end
you get hangovers
the size of small planets
you drink kale smoothies
with bits of leaves
not entirely blended
sticking to the side of the glass
you don't go where you are supposed to go
you are a late kid
you are an early adult
you are the patron saint
of skipping class
you are confident that there
is no deadline you have not missed
you rummage through your pockets
and only find stones
you are restless manic energy
you are loved by the stars too fondly
to stay in one place
you know you are a handful
you know you unravel easily

you know you break constantly
you hypothesize that the reason why
your parents do not love you
as much as your siblings
has to do with this
has to do with all of this and more
but they do not see how your eyes
light up when you talk about the things
you love
they do not hear your voice
carry the words of your poetry
they do not see how you cradle others
they do not see you piece yourself
together with care by moonlight
they do not see you how those who
love you with fierce determination
and without compromise see you
you are as vast and unfathomable
as the sky and their inability to
grasp you does not diminish your value
you owe no explanations
you owe no apologies
you are you
and you continue to stay you
even when their eyes are closed

ACKNOWLEDGEMENTS

The poetry you hold in your hands was brought to you by every winter that reluctantly turned to spring. These poems owe their existence to my friends that have encouraged me to stay here and to keep writing.

I would like to thank Dorian Manuel for their genuine excitement for everything I have produced.

I am honored to thank Alyssa Balzano, who has taught me that unconditional love does indeed exist.

Here's to the gender outlaws and queer heroes who have taught me how to be at home in this body.

Special thanks to Sharp Mesa Vista Hospital for believing in my recovery and helping me translate it all in to words.

Finally, I thank *Black Napkin Press* for providing a platform that actively rebels against the cisheteronormative lens and for allowing my voice to be heard.

Thank you to the following journals who first gave versions of these poems a home:

Hooligan Magazine: "Enmeshment"

The Black Napkin: "as though breathing exercise could cure me of my childhood," "a bouquet of oleander," "our bones are stained with the worst of it," "Lost Boy / Good Girl," and "can you be both the exhibitionist and the voyeur?"

ABOUT THE AUTHOR

Lucas Daliah Galvin (they/them) is a queer disaster always on the prowl for the next dog to pet. They are the patron saint of skipping class. Their work has appeared in *The Black Napkin* and *Hooligan Magazine*. Galvin's work was nominated for the 2016 Best of Net Anthology. When they are not plagued with symptoms of their mental illness, they enjoy rollerskating. They are currently haunting the streets of San Diego.

Black Napkin Press is a 501(c)(3) non-profit organization founded in 2016 to support emerging poets and visual artists. We are committed to disrupting the heteronormative white-cis-male-centric publishing industry by publishing and promoting the work of artists from across the spectrum of cultures, races, religions, ethnicities, and gender/sexual identities. We take a three fold system approach to promotion in the form of an online poetry journal, a print chapbook series, and live poetry performances.

Want to learn more about Black Napkin Press, our authors, or our online publication *The Black Napkin*? Visit us online at:

www.black-napkin-press.com

www.ingramcontent.com/pod-product-compliance
Lightning Source LLC
Chambersburg PA
CBHW020950090426
42736CB00010B/1352